UNTITLED

Echo of emotions ♡

Vanshika Chhabra

BookLeaf
Publishing

India | USA | UK

Dedication

NOTE FROM THE AUTHOR:

Writing is not a skill but an emotion to me. It is something that comes naturally to me. I write in the moment when I feel an emotion or have an experience. Today, everything has gotten complex - Relationships, work life , personal life and much more. In this humdrum, we process our emotions differently and hesitate to admit some. Amidst all of this, we crave for validation. I really hope that my poems soothe your heart and give you the validation that you are not alone in this.

We are together . Hence, my collection is called Untitled as I have left every piece to the interpretation of the reader. This collection is indeed straight from my heart and is a mix of lighthearted, relatable, and thought-provoking themes. Just like mine, I hope your story too finds a place in them.

Let's have a little heart to heart through these pieces ♡

Preface

The feelings so often felt but not put into words...they find their place in these poems. Each poem is an attempt to delve deep into hearts and find place to stay. Covering myriads of relatable themes, this collection is perfect to sit with a cup of coffee and smile to all close bonds dealt with. Maybe it stirs a string or so and make you hug your loved ones after reading them.

Happy Reading ♡

Acknowledgements

A note to my Family: My driving force
I want to come out of your shadow but be your reflection
always !

1. PEARLS OF OUR LIFESTRING:

Personifying grace, our queens own their throne,
It is because of them we call our house a home.
Standing vivaciously through it all,
They are available at our beck and call.

I wish I could always be the little baby in my mama's
lap,
I wish she could always be by my side to guide me
through every map,
For there is no love greater than that of a mother,
No friendship as that of a sister
No warmth as that of a grandmother
And no care as that of a wife
A blessing indeed, we are fortunate enough to have them
in our lives.

In the times so rough,
The ones who stand tall and tough,
The ones to shower us with their unconditional love,

Yet, we fail to thank them enough.
Not a mark of fear or fright,
These women are indeed strength exemplified.
Bold and beautiful, embracing every scar,
The women of our house have made us who we are.
Through years of growing,
Wrapped in comfort,they are the voice that has kept us
going.
In my life, each one plays an important part.
The women in my life will forever be at the core of my
heart.

2. FROM US TO YOU ♡ (From two daughters to their father)

The definition of world for us,
The one who held our hands each day to drop us to the
school bus...
Indeed, a gem who fulfils each of our wishes at the drop
of a hat,
Is..
Our number one superhero...Our Dad
The day he held us in his arm,
Our minds had an affirmation that the world could do us
no harm.
He embraces his queen,
He protects his princesses from the unforeseen ...
A man of indomitable strength and a demeanor that
surprises us all,
Living away, not a day goes by without his phone call.
Always with pride, he broadens his chest...
We are indeed blessed with the best.

The one who adds joy to the days so sad

Is...

Our number one superhero...Our Dad!!

3. HOME-The word screams comfort ♡

Plethora of memories, a treasurer of our jovial glory
days,
A house I call home is my happy place.
Where every corner screams comfort in its own ways,
A humble abode which mama papa made in into safe
space.
When my heart yearns for a mother's hug,
Or I want to sip hot chocolate from my favorite mug,
Or When I fear the unknown,
I escape and rush home...
In the times I feel happy and, in the times, I feel alone,
My escape is a way to my home.
Home is what gives meaning to love and care,
A piece of my heart forever resides in there .

4. A MEMORABLE Wedding Day : (IRONY)

While getting ready for my wedding, my father came in,
His traumatized face giving an expression of him
committing a sin,
He was drenched in sweat that day,
My wedding already being in the month of May.
The collywobbles in my tummy sprang to another level
seeing him that way,
Neither he moved nor a word did he say.
My groom was standing behind my father,
With a frown on his face, he looked miserable rather.
When he came close and removed his hat,
Transfixed in my chair, I sat.
Was all ready and up dolled,
Sat aghast, I saw that my groom was bald.

5. HER :

A little girl,
whose hair had a curl,
whose skin was brown,
who lived in a shanty little town,
fell asleep gazing at a single star,
which from her world was afar...
The dreams in her eyes gleamed bright,
but fulfilling them was out of her sight.
She lived in a dusty world so blur,
yet the hope to come out of the rat hole always resided
in HER!
Each passing night, she fell asleep gazing at a single star,
which from her world was afar !

6. TINY TOES AGAINST THE WORLD:

Warm and tender, gentle and mild,
Innocence can be found within the heart of a child.
With no pessimism around,
Surrounded by an aura so profound.
Estranged to the outside world,
Protected in the arms of the mother, a child stays curled.
Just a tinge of laughter on a child's face,
Is for someone, an eternal solace.
A phase as beautiful as a rose,
Childhood is a chapter we wish to never close.

7. THIRSTY DOG IN THE NASTY BOG:

Running, growling, and howling came the thirsty dog,
To me when I was stuck in the nasty bog.
Water water was all what he wanted,
He was ardent on his thought undaunted.
Mutual help was the only solution left,
Of energy, we both were bereft.
Out of the draggled mess, he pulled a rope,
Pulling me out of the bog was the only hope.
In the helter skelter situation, I was wrenched out,
It was quiet a strenuous operation for me being very
stout.
I took the dog along and found the way home,
Fed the thirsty dog who went on his way leaving me
alone.
A unique bond struck between us two,
His memory faded day by day as the wind blew.
UNTIL...
A few days later, I saw him outside my house bidding the
world his adieu.

8. TESTING COVID POSITIVE!

After spending months protecting ourselves from the
tiny bug, eating and drinking God knows what,
It extended its trap and in it, we were caught.
Standing brave and tall,
Could not prevent it from entering our bodies after all!!
Revenge was its but the battle was ours,
No cure made us think that this strenuous devious bug
had come from Mars.
Being entirely locked in,
made us feel as if we had committed a sin.
A regular cold and cough became a matter if worry,
Out plain sailing life was turned topsy turvy.
Coughing and sneezing didn't stop,
Loss of smell and taste was cherry on top.
Being in quarantine seemed a task,
wandering about in our own house now required a mask.
A tiny germ put a halt to the usual din,
With grit and vigor, we made it a win win.
Finally came the day of the covid test,

As an answer to all our prayers, covid was finally put to
rest!

9. THE GREAT STALLON MANOR :

Written in blood on the walls of Stallon Manor,
is the tale of a wedding planner,
whose lunatic wife sits by the bay,
and recites it all day.
The love that became as toxic as weed,
diverted her to move on the path of greed.
She poisoned her man,
to hide the dead body, the maniac had a perfect plan.
Buried alive, under the garden of Stallon Manor,
is Mr. Sengupta-the dear departed wedding planner.
The lunatic wife did not get a penny,
Mr. Sengupta, in his will, had given everything to his
lover Jenny.

10. LIVING IN THE UNCERTAIN :

Life today has become uncertain-a gamble of breath.
We no longer hold a map to our journey. All our paths
have become twisted and what lies ahead are
blind turns. Every ounce of our breath is precious, and
we attempt to preserve it forever. However,
the sea of life one day finds its shore. So, perceive and
absorb every miniscule breath to the fullest.
We never know what lies ahead of us-roses or thorns,
rainbows, or storm. Every moment is
magnificent because you have the breath to live it and
senses to feel it.
SO...
TILL THE TIME YOU'RE BREATHING......LIVE !

11. PERFECTION:

There is a baggage we carry our entire lives and it is that
of PERFECTION. The word PERFECTION
equals pressure which fills up to the saturation point and
a human head intends to explode.
LIFE IS TOO SHORT TO JUST BE PERFECT.
EMBRACE YOUR IMPERFECTIONS BECAUSE THEY
MAKE YOU PERFECT.
In today's world, it is only the gold that glimmers and
diamonds that sparkle. Only the imaginary
world is painted pink. The reality has its innumerable
shades-hues of both despair and joy.
Perfection is simply a hypothetical and non-existent for
no one till date has had the ability to attain it.
In the humdrum of today, perfection has become the
finish line to this mad rat race nobody can ever
win. YET...the chase to it never ends.

12. DILEMMA :

One day we live,
On the other, we simply thrive,
On to the next, we wish to just survive
AND WITH THIS,
We continue to pass through days, weeks, and years
BECAUSE,
Life is a dilemma.

13. ANXIETY:
YOU ARE NOT ALONE
(In this battle of life, we should all be there for each other as anxiety is experienced by all)

THEY SAY ,
"Breathe in breathe out"-a temporary relief and in no
time it's back again.
In a room filled with people, my heart feels desolated
and what stays aloof within me is a daily dose
of anxiety. People become my foe and loneliness my
friend. My mind wanders for answers to this
inexplicable restlessness. Maybe it is a baggage from our
past, a personal trauma or an experience
that creates a void which is then filled up by anxiety.
Answers are many but SOLUTIONS.. NONE.

In sickness or in health, anxiety is an emotion we all
tend to experience in our own ways. We laugh,
cry, or detonate. Customarily...anxiety is at its service. It
shatters you from within, puts you down and
turns your smile into a frown.
In the most peaceful setting, my heart beating faster than
ever and its sound reaching my ears tell
me to run. And the tingling sensation in my stomach,
making me want to throw up. I wish I could kick
it out of my system. But, anxiety always wins over.
Dear Anxiety,
No matter how much I try to escape your sounding
effects, you will always be present in a discreet
corner of my heart.
IN THIS BATTLE OF LIFE,
YOU ARE NOT ALONE!

14. WAILING VOICE OF A PRISONER:

I am a normal one, I too have a heart,
It hurts to the core when the police beat each of my body part.
My inner self yells being locked up in a cage,
Time passes by and my body just grows older in age.
Seeing my family, I pray for their forgiveness, yet a faint smile lightens up my face,
For a miniscule period, my problems go efface.
Dingy cells, stale food and not a ray of light,
Every fraction of second adds up to the fright.
Awaiting a miracle, let me free is what I say all day,
In here, a cost for our crimes, we pay.
Just darkness prevails around,
Entire day, all I can hear is the policemen hound.
Not a false ray of hope seems to be left,
what an irrevocable mistake of mine to engage myself in theft.
As days pass by, my heart sobs more and more,

Torn apart, dead from within, I wish I could exit this prison door.

15. SILENCE :

Silence prevails around,
the beauty in it remains unfound.
For silence is never silent,
It is reverent.
The peace in it echoes
and the beauty in it remains undiscovered.
Sometimes horrifying, sometimes alluring,
each time it possesses a distinct meaning.
Hidden in happiness and in pain,
Silence is found in every drop
of rain.
Silence is indeed the biggest speaker,
For when silence speaks, it shuts them all.

16. FOR A MOMENT THERE, I LOST MYSELF:

Amidst the nature, in the rain,
Walking on a mountainous terrain.
The soft touch of the cold breeze on my face,
And all my despairs go efface.
Silently sitting and gazing at the beauty around,
My ears absorbing the encircling sounds.
Of wind striking against the tress.
And falling withering leaves.
Rays of the sun kissing my face,
Seeing the cotton candy like clouds bring eternal solace.
An unfound peace striking my mind numb,
Nature has its beauty even in the tiniest crumb.
To find myself, I run through its chaos,
In every essence of its, I get lost...

17. FLOWERS :
Beauty that blooms

The beauty in them remains submerged,
The colors in them diverged.
Each color presents forth a different mood,
They are a source of life, for their nectar is bee's food.
Their aroma inexplicably astounding,
Even their silence adorns the surrounding.
Looking at them is a joyous celebration,
they are god's beatific creation.
Sitting still, every corner they grace,
Calm and composed they stand in a vase,
Holding them, a lover kneels down,
Perfect to embellish a queen's crown,
Always around, yet their presence remains unfound.

18. UP THERE:

The skies above dwell upon a single thought,
One day, all humans will rot,
In heaven or hell,
Casted upon us is god's vicious spell.
The moon, sun, and stars,
Staring at us from a world afar.
Every single day is someone's number,
Whose sleep shall pass into a forever slumber.
UP THERE IS, FROM WHERE,
EVERYTHING VANISHES INTO THIN AIR.
The world from there is a tiny place,
With this I move on and rest my case.

19. FINDING YOURSELF:
All the roads will eventually lead you to YOURSELF!

It is very easy to break the broken but much more
difficult to build the broke. Hope is as frail as an
old woman. The moment you drop it, you lose hold of it.
At times, I wish to just pause my life or rewind it or fast
forward it to see what the future holds. But
in a blink of an eye, this hazy dream of mine unfolds into
reality. Time never stops. What is gone is
gone and what is ahead is going to happen no matter
what. There is no magic wand to control life.
Cut the past, shut the future and you will have the key to
the present. Live in the moment.
In this myriads of feelings and gush of emotions, you are
yet to be found and you can be the only one
to find yourself.
LIFE IS ALL ABOUT MAKING CHOICES UNTIL YOU
MAKE THE RIGHT ONE.
Life is a sea of opportunities. Learn to swim. Be the one

to row your own boat.

You might have to go fathoms deep or take several roads.

Eventually ... They will lead up to YOU...

20. UNSPOKEN VOICE WITHIN

Standing there,
I listen and hear,
And my words find no voice,
Suppressed under dominance, they find no choice..
Enforced upon,
Are a hundred questions
And I gave answers to none.
Not being able to find a way,
I chose to run.

21. TALE OF LIFE :

Life offers many phases
A phase once crossed never comes back
Accept each broken bond as a passed phase of your life
For a new chapter begins thereafter
Presenting forth another story...
Each chapter has its own beauty
Reliving it is nearly impossible
So live each moment because it is as precious as a pearl.
PHASES COME AND GO
AND
HENCEFORTH,THE TALE CONTINUES.

22. IT SHALL PASS :

We assume that the knot of pain always remains taut.
But with time passing by, it loosens up and it
hurts less. Eventually, the dust settles and the season
shifts from autumn to spring and there is
transition from darkness to light. At some point, you see
everything spring to life, adding some color
to your mundane. But it is YOU who has to travel
through the tunnel in order to reach to the end to
get a glimpse of the sun.
In the world of today sunken in its humdrum and chaos,
we need to put a comma in our lives. Life
does not need a full stop but just a comma because in
this ongoing rat race, we ought to find a
moment for ourselves to gain inner peace and solace else
we will lose ourselves to the world we
might not even know. A brief pause keeps you afloat and
keeps you on the never-ending road to
success.
Rushing towards achieving more and more without
taking a moment to relish what we have pushes

us into a void. Unnecessarily, carrying on the weight-the
baggage of dejections and disappointments
never fills the void rather increases the vacuum, thus
creating a domino effect. Little moments of joy
if not taken for granted lift you up from a state of
despondence and gloom.
At times, just leave it to the gods above for everything
happens for a REASON,
It is his wish...be it the summer, winter, or monsoon
SEASON!

23. UNTITLED:

Reassemble your widespread thoughts,
For they may have become treacherous clots.
Calm yourself and relax your brain,
For it may unclean like a lion's mane.
Shut the doors of the future and eradicate the
reminiscences of the past,
For the present is what remains atlast.
Make the worst thoughts cease to exist,
Live it at heart...grasp it in your fist.
Take the essence of every second for time runs very fast,
Live every moment for any day could possible be your
last.

24. LOVE :

When my mood is sinking,
Love keeps me afloat.
When my lips frown,
Love turns it upside down.
When my heart cries,
Love wipes down the tears rolling down my eyes...
When I wish to pour my heart out without fear,
Love lends me an ear.
When my life isn't easy going,
Love keeps me flowing.
When my anxiety pops.
Love puts it to stop.
Love joins the pieces of my puzzle,
Love is my calm in the hustle bustle.
Love is not a single relation.
But a feeling of comfort and elation.
LOVE is always pure,
To any ailment, love is the simplest CURE.

25. GOODBYE- Preserving memories and moving onto the next chapter .

A gesture of parting ways,
with a place, person or phase,
heart in sombre, a thousand emotions it conveys.
Leaving behind memories of the days gone by,
the heart still stuck in time, refusing to move on gives a
loud cry.
Last tight hug to the loved ones and gratitude to the
experiential learning-
the heart wails,
and through a goodbye, a thousand emotions it conveys.
A pending hope to meet again,
A melancholic spell of unending pain.
Goodbye- an emotion one can never explain.